PHILIP W...
CA..
CRUSHER

Illustrated by
George Buchanan

OXFORD
UNIVERSITY PRESS

HEMPSTEAD C. P. SCHOOL
JUNIOR DEPARTMENT

OXFORD
UNIVERSITY PRESS

Great Clarendon Street, Oxford OX2 6DP

Oxford University Press is a department of the University of Oxford.
It furthers the University's objective of excellence in research, scholarship,
and education by publishing worldwide in

Oxford New York

Athens Auckland Bangkok Bogotá Buenos Aires Calcutta
Cape Town Chennai Dar es Salaam Delhi Florence Hong Kong Istanbul
Karachi Kuala Lumpur Madrid Melbourne Mexico City Mumbai
Nairobi Paris São Paulo Shanghai Singapore Taipei Tokyo Toronto Warsaw

and associated companies in Berlin Ibadan

Oxford is a trade mark of Oxford University Press
in the UK and in certain other countries

Text © Philip Wooderson 2001
The moral rights of the author have been asserted
Database right Oxford University Press (maker)
First published 2001

All rights reserved
No part of this publication may be reproduced,
stored in a retrieval system, or transmitted, in any form or by any means,
without the prior permission in writing of Oxford University Press,
or as expressly permitted by law, or under terms agreed with the appropriate
reprographics rights organisation. Enquiries concerning reproduction
outside the scope of the above should be sent to the Rights Department,
Oxford University Press, at the address above

You must not circulate this book in any other binding or cover
and you must impose this same condition on any acquiror

British Library Cataloguing in Publication Data
Data available

ISBN 0 19 915966 1

Printed in the UK by Ebenezer Baylis & Son Ltd

Available in packs

Year 6 / Primary 7 Pack of Six (one of each book) ISBN 0 19 915971 8
Year 6 / Primary 7 Class Pack (six of each book)   ISBN 0 19 915972 6

Contents

1 Something is Wrong 5
2 Deeper and Deeper 10
3 Ahmed's Bribe 15
4 The Camera Can't Lie 23
5 No Wages for Ahmed 30
6 The Spray Team 42
7 Phoning the Police 55
8 Wheels within Wheels 66
9 Brains at Work 73
10 Sully and Sty Give a Hand 86
11 Explanations 91
About the author 94

1
Something is Wrong

I knew there was something wrong as soon as I opened the door.

Mum finished work early on Thursdays so she was usually home before I got back from school. But when I called out, "Hi, Mum," there was no reply. "Anyone in?" I called again and went into the kitchen.

There she was at the table, reading the evening paper.

"Hey, Mum?"

Still no reply. Feeling a bit annoyed, I imitated her voice: "Oh, hello, Neil. Have a good day? Not bad, Mum. Thanks for asking."

But Mum didn't even smile. I tried to look over her shoulder.

The picture on the front page was of a smashed-up car. The headline read:

**SHOCK FOR SHOPPERS AS
JOYRIDER RAMS SUPERMARKET**

Mum moved a bit to the left, and I read the whole piece about a stolen car crashing through the plate-glass window of the Super Save in our High Street, on Saturday afternoon. *Police are eager to question the driver who is still in intensive care, suffering from head injuries.*

This was dramatic stuff, but didn't explain Mum's silence. Was she upset about something?

"Did you know anyone who was hurt, Mum?"

She turned and gave me a tight smile, her eyes as sharp as needles. Not much in itself maybe, but I knew enough about Mum to hear alarm bells clanging.

"Tell me, Neil, what you were doing last Saturday afternoon."

I did my best to remember. Saturday had been boring, except I'd watched the big match on telly while Mum had been out at work, doing her weekend shift. Most Saturday afternoons I went round to Gran's, but last weekend she had been away on a coach trip, up in the Lake District somewhere.

"Apart from the football?" I said. "Arsenal played at home and they'd have beaten Man U, except for one crucial offside by—"

"Nee-ill." (Danger signal number two was when Mum stretched my name and managed to break it in half.)

"I'm answering what you asked, Mum. I'm saying I watched telly."

She glared at me. "Telly? Weren't you watching the match somewhere else?"

"Ha, ha, Mum. You mean at the ground?"

"And that's just a joke, is it, Neil?"

A very bad joke, I thought, after what happened a couple of weeks before, the only time in two years I'd got to a real live match.

But I couldn't say that now, not with Mum so angry.

She went on quietly, "No, Neil. You did it again, didn't you? Last time, I only found out you'd slipped off to the match because you got caught up in a riot and I was home first."

What was going on? Mum was watching me, waiting for me to reply.

"You think I went to the match last Saturday?" I said slowly.

"Didn't you?" Mum said.

"How could I? Listen, Mum, I spent Gran's birthday money on the other match. I'm practically skint at the moment!"

"So how do you explain *that*?" she snapped. Now she was pointing her finger hard at a picture captioned: **FANS RUN AMOK**.

I looked. The picture showed a fan dangling from a mesh fence, with two more rival fans hanging on to his legs, trying to pull him down. It did look a bit... familiar.

"Recognize someone?" she prompted. "Down in the bottom right corner?"

A couple more fans were watching, mouths

open as if they were shouting.

Okay, so one was Ahmed and – the other one looked like – me.

"Now what do you say?" said Mum.

"I... wasn't there."

"You're lying!"

2
Deeper and Deeper

I told Mum I couldn't believe what was happening. It was like a bad dream, I said, having my face in the paper when: "I promise you, Mum, hand on heart, I watched that match at home! If you don't trust me, ask Ahmed."

"Perhaps your friends tell lies too?"

"Ahmed wouldn't need to," I fired back.

"And why would that be, I wonder?"

I took a deep breath. Dodgy ground this. "His dad doesn't mind if he goes to matches, Mum. I mean, he's an Arsenal fan too. He even buys Ahmed tickets."

Mum nodded grimly. "I get it. This is all my fault because I've not got the money to pay for football tickets."

"You're twisting my words!" I exploded, grabbing hold of the paper and staring at my own face in that horrible picture. "I'm sorry, but I just don't understand this!"

"I do," Mum said. "You deceived me. And what's more, from that picture it looks as if you got caught up in the worst sort of hooliganism. For all I know, you were involved too. For all I know, the police are after you at this moment!"

"Oh, Mum, that's ridiculous!"

"Is it? I really don't know any more. But I'm not letting it rest, Neil. I think I might phone Ahmed's dad."

"Do that!" I yelled and hunkered out of the kitchen, slamming the door so hard it banged and bounced open again. As I stomped up the stairs, I heard her call: "Bully boy tactics!"

Thanks Mum. I was the one feeling bullied.

I threw myself down on the bed.

* * *

I started thinking about the one and only match I had ever been to. Two weeks ago last Saturday, Mum had just left for work when Ahmed had phoned to say he'd got a spare ticket for the Arsenal game. It had been a great offer. The ticket had been half-price and I'd bought it with my birthday money.

It wasn't my fault we were late back because some fans got a bit out of hand. That's all it was. Not a riot. But yes, I had promised to ask her before I went to any more matches. And I'd kept my side of the bargain.

Now I heard her come up the stairs. I heard her come into my room. I heard her say, "Well, I've phoned him. I got him on his mobile."

I looked away and then I heard myself say, "Satisfied?"

She pulled in her breath. "Ahmed's dad says you went to that match."

It took me a moment to hear this. I rolled

over. "What was that, Mum?"

"You went with Ahmed," she said. "Ahmed's dad says he bought you a ticket."

My jaw dropped. "What? That's not right, Mum."

"You're saying *he's* telling me lies now?"

"You must be making this up!"

"How dare you!" She was close to tears.

I was bewildered. I scrambled up off the

bed and raced downstairs. I couldn't see anything clearly.

"Where do you think you're off to?"

"I'm going to see Ahmed's dad!"

3
Ahmed's Bribe

Ahmed's dad made lots of money running a motor-parts business. He loved fast cars and football. Ahmed did too. So did I. But I wasn't thinking of that as I stormed up their long drive.

I was nearly at the front door when I heard gravel scrunching behind me. I spun round to see a black Jaguar nosing through the gateway. The electric window slid down and Ahmed's dad was grinning. "Hey, hello there, Neil. Enjoy the match on Saturday?"

I stared at him. Was he playing some sort

of joke? "What did
you tell my Mum?"

He thumbed a tab on
the dashboard, and the garage door swung
slowly up and over, revealing the silver Lancia
Ahmed's mum sported around in. "I could
only tell her what Ahmed's found time to tell
me. Great game and you had a great time. Just
a pity we didn't win, eh?" He winked and
nudged his right foot down, sending the car
powering forwards into the open garage.

I didn't hang about. Keeping my hand on
the door bell until the door opened, I blurted
at Ahmed's mum that I had to see Ahmed
at once.

She wrinkled her nose doubtfully, "He's busy now doing his homework."

Did she really believe that? Muttering an excuse, I slipped straight past her, heading for Ahmed's room where I found him on the computer, playing SPACE WARS 3.

He gave me a casual grin (as smooth as his dad, I thought). But it faded out double-quick when he saw how angry I was.

"What's the matter?" he demanded.

I told him about my mum getting in such a state. "And now your dad's gone and told her all sorts of amazing stuff about how he paid for my ticket. He thinks I went to the match. I've just met him. I want to know what's going on!"

Ahmed turned back to his keyboard and shut down the game. "Slight glitch at my end," he said quietly, looking at the blank screen.

"Would you like to explain?" I suggested.

Ahmed took his time, leaning back in his seat. "It was just... I had to tell Dad... that you and I went to the match together."

"Had to?"

"To keep him sweet."

"Why?"

Ahmed held up his hands with all his fingers splayed out. "He bought a couple of tickets, and he very generously said you could have one of them, Neil."

"You mean I ought to have thanked him?"

"Well, to be polite and all that..."

"But I didn't go! I mean, Ahmed. You didn't even invite me!"

"Bad luck, Neil, but I missed out too."

"Ahmed!" I grabbed his shoulders and swivelled him round in his chair. "You've got me into a bad mess. My mum's raving mad. She's convinced I'm a thug who's been telling her lies. You've got to tell her the truth, now!"

He shut his eyes. "Neil, I can't do that."

I stared at him. "Can't or won't?"

And then he poured it all out. "Listen, Neil, I had to do it. You know my Saturday job, down at Brains the car breakers? It's a great job, and he pays well, but my dad doesn't like it at all. He hates Brains because Brains sells second-hand parts salvaged out of old cars, right? He's under-cutting my dad. And you don't know my dad. He's sweet as can be on the outside, but don't try and cross him. You with me?"

I shook my head angrily. "Ahmed, you've lost me. What has this got to do with—"

"I'm telling you." He wiped his forehead, as if he was suddenly hot. "Dad gave me those football tickets, as a sort of a bribe because he wants me to stop working for Brains. He knew how much I wanted to go to the match. And I *would* have gone if it hadn't meant losing my job. When I asked Brains if I could have the afternoon off, he got really nasty about it. He moaned that he wanted to go off somewhere himself. He said he needed me there until five. That or get sacked. I didn't have a choice."

Ahmed avoided looking at me. "Sorry you missed the game, Neil, but I couldn't have missed the game myself and given you a ticket. Would have doubled the pain. There it is."

I stared at him. "Where is what?" I said coldly.

"If I tell your mum," said Ahmed uncomfortably, "she'll tell my dad. He'll go crazy and when my dad goes crazy, you have to take cover. It's scary. Like twenty times more scary than your crazy mum going crazy. Listen, you know what I'll do, Neil? I'll give you the cash for that ticket."

I hit him. It wasn't much of a punch, glancing off his chin, but it left a red blotch.

Ahmed was too amazed to hit back which was lucky for me, because Ahmed's bigger than I am. He just rubbed the red mark with the tips of his fingers and blinked. "Wow! Have I mis-diagnosed this?"

We both took a moment to wonder. Then I

told him about the picture in the local paper.

"You must have a double then, Neil."

"Me?" I managed to smile back. "If you didn't go to the match, you shouldn't have been in it, either."

He blinked. "If I *am* in it, there must have been a mistake."

"What sort of mistake can you think of?"

He frowned. "I'm wondering. I think I see what has happened."

"Okay, why not tell me?" I said.

Ahmed folded his arms and looked at the ceiling again. "The picture must have been taken before, at the match we really went to. In fact I can even remember, near the end, after that goal kick, that some silly wally did try to get over the fence."

It was the obvious answer and my first reaction was a twinge of resentment that I'd not thought of it before. Straightaway, in fact, when Mum had showed me the picture. I shrugged doubtfully. "Mum's not going to swallow that, Ahmed. I've got to prove it, somehow."

"So, check it out. Take her the facts."

"What facts? There aren't any facts!"

But Ahmed was back to his old, cool self. In a casual way he said that one of his elder cousins had a job on the sports' desk at the evening paper. "Might give her a call," he said, swinging his swivel-chair round so he could click a few keys and get back into his game.

"Might?"

"On one condition. You swear and hope to die, you won't tell my dad."

4
The Camera Can't Lie

When I got to school the next morning, there was a police car outside. Nobody seemed to know why, but there were lots of jokes. Everyone said it was because Ahmed and I had been caught in a riot at Saturday's match.

All the teachers had noticed our photo in the evening paper. Even the dinner ladies had seen it; but at least they thought it was funny. Not like our headteacher, whose heavy hand gripped my shoulder as I came out of lunch.

"I've just seen the paper, Neil!"

"I wasn't there, Mr Hotblack."

He took a step back, frowning. "Oh, really? It looks very much as if you *were* there. And that other lad looks exactly like your chum, Ahmed. But Ahmed has got the sense not to deny it. So you're telling me that the camera is lying, is that right? Or have you got a twin brother?"

"No, sir, but—" What was the point? Except if I let this pass, he might tell my mum I'd admitted I'd been at the match. "There's been a mistake, sir."

He let out a high-pitched bark. "Mistake? So you think it's a joke, do you?"

"Me, sir?"

"Yes, you, sir! How d'you think I felt when the police asked if those two louts featured in the paper were pupils from this school? I couldn't deny it. How could I?"

He glared at me. "I don't hold any high hopes, boy, about you being charged, not this time, at least. But I'm warning you. If the police start asking questions, don't try any silly games. Speak the truth or you'll be in deep water."

I was speechless.

His expression relaxed a little.

"I'll set you a challenge," he said. "Next time you get in the papers, make sure it's for something good. But I warn you, it's not quite so easy." Then his secretary called him to say a school governor had just arrived for "the meeting", and he walked away. But I was properly rattled.

I found Ahmed out in the yard. He grinned. "He's having you on, Neil. The police came because of his car."

I sighed with relief. "What about it?"

Ahmed filled me in: "You know that Escort he drives, the XR4 with the alloy wheels? Someone's pinched them. He left it parked in the street outside his house on Friday night, and when he woke up in the morning, the car was left mounted on bricks!"

I shouldn't have laughed, but I did.

* * *

That was the one bright moment in the whole dreadful day.

Back home, Mum was still seething. When the phone rang, she answered and I heard her say, "Listen, Ahmed, I don't want you taking Neil to any more football matches. I'm going to pay your dad back for the ticket he bought for the last one and Neil will have to refund me out of his paper-round money. Got that?" Her lips tightened. "Good. Now I'll hand you over."

I'd got it all right. It was not good. Three weeks of paper rounds to pay for a match I'd not been to! I snatched the phone. "Yes, Ahmed?"

"Ah hi, I'm... sorry about that."

"I bet. Have you talked to your cousin on the sports' desk yet?"

"Yes, but now it turns out she works in another department. I mean, she's not anywhere near the sports' desk. She's selling classified ads for second-hand cars and vans; but I got her to make some enquiries. Nobody from the paper took that picture, because it was shot on the terrace, up in the crowd. So that means it was a freelance."

"Big deal," I said.

"Wait, there's more. She checked and the picture was handed in on Saturday evening—"

"Who by? I interrupted.

"They couldn't say who he was. He left no name or address. He just came back

on Monday morning and got paid cash for the picture. And the person who handled it all is off for the rest of the week. But I've got a really good blow-up of the original photo."

"Oh, very big deal," I said.

"No, don't you be like that, Neil. I think you should come round and see it. I think I've got a new lead. I've a hunch we might sort this all out."

As I put the phone down I felt Mum's eyes still on me. I looked round. She managed a smile. "Let's be friends again, Neil." She touched my wrist with her hand. "Just own up and we can forget it and talk about something else."

I shut my eyes tight. "Sorry, Mum, I – I've… got to go out and see Ahmed."

She turned away without a word, which saved me from making excuses. No talk about how late it was, or how it was dark outside, or whether I'd finished my homework, although I still felt bad, walking out of the flat, knowing I'd left her thinking I was not only a liar, but stubborn too.

Well, I'd show her.

* * *

As I turned into the drive, Ahmed stepped out from the pillar by the front gate.

"Go no further. I want you to come with me."

"Hold on. What about this photo?"

"I'll show you when we get down there."

"Where?"

"Where I work. Brains the Breakers."

5
No Wages for Ahmed

Brains' yard was half a mile down the busy main road, then left, past a dead-end sign, along a dark narrow street with potholes full of brown water, to an iron gate at the far end. A single spluttering street lamp leaned at an angle towards a sign on the fence which announced in faded letters: BRAINS' BREAKERS – Car wrecks welcome.

Ahmed decided he needed to fill me in, and he kept up a commentary on how Brains managed his business, paying just a few pounds for cars delivered to him, or offering to come and tow them away for free. Brains ransacked the cars for spare parts and crushed whatever was left into a slab of scrap to be sold to the smelting works. "He does fifty cars a week here."

"And what do you do?" I said.

"Me? I tidy things up."

It didn't look wonderfully tidy. Litter was stuck in the mesh fence, and a pile of broken car doors stacked inside the gate, was toppled all over the place, as if they'd been blown by the wind. Another sign on the gate dangled from one hook, so you had to turn your head sideways to read what it said, which was: DOGS! And then in small faded letters, buried in blotches of rust: *You Have Been Warned. Keep out.*

I could hear dogs barking, but they seemed to be safely shut up in one of the sheds. At least, they were throwing themselves hard at the metal door, and so far they hadn't smashed through it. I glanced at Ahmed. He grinned. "Don't look so worried. It's fine!"

The yard was crowded with car wrecks

jammed so close to each other, you couldn't have opened a door. Further back, they were piled in heaps up to four or five high, and as the wind blew in cold gusts across the open space, we could hear them creak as they rocked about, like yachts with steel rigging bobbing about in a harbour.

Ahmed showed me a mound of tyres. "That's what I did last weekend. Them and those exhaust pipes."

The exhaust pipes were stacked like logs, a very neat bit of work. There were skips full of batteries and big, rusty drums oozing oil, staining the ground slimy black, and even a hole in the ground, like an open burial site, piled with old, torn car seats, their springs pointing out at odd angles.

Ahmed said his dad had come to collect him about a month ago, and not had the nerve to drive in, so he'd left his Jag in the road. "Brains came out of a shed in his oily overalls, with his hands and face all smeared and his hair standing up like horns! Dad practically bolted," said Ahmed. "When he'd got back in

the car, he said: 'If cars go to hell when they die, this is it – Brains' yard!'"

I looked at the sheds more closely. They stretched in a ramshackle line of different heights, all made of bits of metal held together with iron pins bashed into wooden frames and painted matt black. The biggest shed was at the end, with a curved roof like an aircraft hanger. Next to it was what looked like a giant guillotine made of black iron girders, supporting a vast block of concrete. "What on earth's that?"

"That over there—" Ahmed pointed. "That's the car crusher, Neil. Brains stacks it with four or five cars. Then he lets down the concrete block and there's a big air compressor that forces it down even further until all the cars are smashed flat. It makes an incredible racket as if they're all screaming in pain!"

Ahmed loved this place. I could see why his Dad was prepared to fork out for football tickets.

"So where's Mr Brains?" I wondered.

"It's not *Mr* Brains. Brains is his nickname. Because he's not clever," said Ahmed. "Dad thinks his name was Brian, but he spelt it wrong on the sign. Then people started calling him Brains and he forgot his real name."

We were outside a shed marked PARTS SHOP. Ahmed rattled the door and a bell clanged. Moments later, we heard wires twanging and then the latch clicked back and the door fell open wide. Inside it was badly lit, reeking of grease and paraffin. I heard a rummaging noise from the far end.

"Yeah, yeah?" It was a woman's voice, though it sounded like rusty hinges. "I'll be with you in a tick."

This gave me time to peer round at all the metal shelves leaning at dangerous angles out from the walls. A lop-sided structure formed a sort of island in the middle and it was loaded with chunks of greasy, black machinery: cylinder heads, whole engines, gear boxes, pumps and axles, all leaking droplets of oil. Brown parcel tags in loopy pencil writing gave the car type and price.

"I'm just coming now," Rusty Hinge called. Next moment she slouched round the island. She was wearing an enormous mauve sweatshirt and tight cream leggings that gave the amazing impression she'd forgotten to put on her jeans and was just wearing flip flops. She wiped greasy hair from her forehead. "It's Ahmed! What brings you here, luv?"

"A couple of things to ask Brains."

She swung round and screeched, "Brainy? Brainy? You're wanted!"

There were rattlings and bangings and crashings. Then Brains emerged, wiping his hands with a rag. He was a small, craggy man, with bushy black eyebrows that met, making a shaggy bump like a huge, furry caterpillar squiggling along his forehead. His arms hunched out with his elbows up, and his hands were like big, grasping claws. His legs were short and squat. He was wearing old overalls that could have stood up without him, they were so stiff with oil and grease.

"Not Saturday is it?" he challenged.

Ahmed agreed about this. "But when I finished work on Saturday, you weren't around, Brains, to pay me."

"That so? No, I weren't around, but how would you know about that?"

"Because I was here," said Ahmed. "That's why I'm owed wages, remember?"

The caterpillar went wiggly. "Got anything else to tell me?"

Ahmed pulled a brown envelope out of his

smart brown leather jacket, and carefully took out the photograph I'd seen in the evening paper. He was right. It was really sharp and you could see every detail, although I still couldn't understand why this would make any difference to anyone, least of all Brains. But Ahmed was showing Brains the two figures in the foreground, the ones who were pulling the fan from the fence.

"I've got a favour to ask, Brains. D'you know where we might find these two? I've seen them here, buying parts."

Brains pawed the photo, leaving dark oily marks. "You're innit and all, aren't you, Ahmed?"

Ahmed was patient. "That's me."

"So—" The caterpillar stretched out and went back to sleep. "I'm not that stupid. I saw the evening paper. That told me something about you. Like where you were on Saturday afternoon. So there's your answer, Ahmed, about your wages."

"What? Sorry?"

"So you should be. For skiving off to that

match as soon as I'd gone. You'd told me you wanted to go. And that's what you did. So, no wages."

Ahmed's face crumpled up.

I couldn't help feeling a whiff of satisfaction, because now he knew how I'd felt.

"But that's why I asked you," he blurted. "Because we think that photo was taken two matches ago. We just need to prove it, somehow."

"If we find those two," I prompted, "we

can ask them which game they went to."

Brains suddenly turned on me. "They might have been at both matches!" He wasn't so stupid after all.

"That's true, but... we'd like to find out. From them. Maybe they know who took the photo."

The caterpillar rolled up into a perfect U.

"You must know their names," Ahmed prodded.

Brains shook his head. "I don't ask names. This business is cash, and no questions. But don't try changing the subject."

"Go and look at my heap of tyres. I was here all afternoon, Brains!"

"Nope. Sorry to say, mate, you're fired."

Ahmed opened his mouth, and closed it again with a gulp. Rusty Hinge let out her breath in a wheeze like a tyre going flat, as if she was feeling let down.

Ahmed turned on his heels. But as soon as the door clanged behind us, he turned back to me with wild eyes. "I never expected all that. It's not fair! What got into him, Neil?"

"That picture," I said. "It's stitched up both of us, now."

"Oh, no," Ahmed said. "We'll sort this. We've got the brains, I mean, real brains. Not like..." He waved at the door.

6
The Spray Team

At break on Thursday morning, I asked Ahmed what bright ideas he'd had in the night. (I'd got nowhere.)

"It's sorted," he said.

"Oh, yes?" I didn't believe him. "And how have you managed to do that? Have you traced those fans by the fence?"

"Yes. Suddenly – wham – I got it. Those two guys in the picture – they came in a van!"

"A van?" I said sarcastically. "A big van or a small van? Think carefully. Could be important."

Ahmed looked irritated. "That van had stuff on the side, Neil."

"Words?" I said.

"Yes." He waved his hands about. "It said: 'Holly Tree Garage'. And there was a telephone number, but I can't remember that bit."

I had to admit this was a lead. We'd easily find the number in the Yellow Pages, if Holly Tree Garage existed.

"No need." He looked pleased with himself now. "I've already talked to my dad. He likes Holly Tree Garage. They buy lots of nice new parts. It's out near the bowling alley. Five stops on the 38 bus."

* * *

We took the bus straight after school and got there soon after five. It was set back from the road with a wide forecourt with flagpoles, filled with second-hand cars that looked brand new to me. But the ones that were really brand new were kept in a glass-fronted show room and these didn't have any prices splattered across their windscreens.

A man in a suit was shuffling his cuffs round his wrists, trying to talk an old lady into buying a ZXi turbo with huge chrome exhausts like machine guns. He wasn't too pleased to have us taking up valuable time.

"Don't touch!" was the first thing he said.

I lifted my fingers from the coupé's snarly front grille, leaving a smudge on the chrome. Then Ahmed pulled his photograph out of the envelope, and pointed out the two figures grappling the fan on the fence. The salesman tilted the picture away from his customer, frowning as if he'd just noticed a scratch on the wing of the coupé.

"Sully and Sty!" he reacted.

"Friends of yours?" Ahmed suggested.

The salesman's face twisted, sourly.

"Or... do they just work here?" I said.

The salesman squeezed his hands in front of his wide striped tie and made an odd noise in his throat.

"Excuse me," said the old lady. "I asked about fuel injection?"

"That's right, ma'am, won't be a moment." He shot me a glance. "Yes, they worked here, in the service department. Until they got sacked."

"What for?"

"Well, they were naughty boys, weren't they?"

Both Ahmed and I leaned closer.

"How were they naughty?" asked Ahmed.

The old lady clacked her tongue. "If you don't want to sell me this car, I'll go across the road and buy an Alfa instead—"

"No, madam—" The salesman looked desperate.

"Just say where we can find them," said Ahmed.

The salesman dashed into the office and came back a moment later with an older man in a more expensive suit. He was holding the photograph.

The boss smirked at me. "Do I take it, they've got themselves into more trouble, up at the football ground?"

"They might have," I said. "We want to find out."

He fingered his nose for a moment, then pulled out a business card and scribbled an address on the back. "You do that. Then give us a bell to let us know what you find out. But don't tell them I sent you!"

* * *

On the way home, Ahmed and I sat on the top deck of the bus, trying to puzzle out what Sty and Sully might have done to get the sack from the garage. The men in suits hadn't told us, only hinted that they could turn nasty.

We got off one stop early and asked in a

corner shop for Burma Mews. It sounded surprisingly posh, but it turned out to be a row of garages behind the main street. We wanted number six and we were in luck. The only garage doors open in the whole yard were at number six. They were orange and splodged with stickers for engine oils and spark plugs. A sign up above said SPRAY TEAM and from inside came a loud hissing noise.

Peering round the doorway, I saw a car without wheels, mounted on wooden trestles, with all its chrome and glass wrapped up in paper and tape. The bodywork was a mixture of blue bits and brown bits and grey bits, with a brilliant yellow back end, thanks to a man in goggles wearing a mask and white overalls, who was spraying away with a paint gun. The paint went on smooth and shiny and it smelt both tangy and sweet.

We were so busy watching, we got a bit of a shock when someone came up behind us and squeezed his hands round the backs of our necks.

I managed to twist round and found myself up so close I could smell his after-shave, mixed up with the leathery smell that came from his black zip-up jacket. He was thin as a whippet, but tall, with hair shaved up the sides leaving a mop of fair hair slicked with gel on top and a long pimply face that was twisted into a nasty grin.

"Hey, Sully. Look what I've got here!"

The paint gun suddenly cut out, leaving the air compressor still hissing away in the background.

Sully lifted his mask. He was soft and fleshy and bald, with eyes like shiny black marbles stuck in a lump of dough. "So, ask what our visitors want, Sty. Offer 'em tea or coffee. You be polite for a change."

Sty let go of our necks. "You heard the man. What you after?"

"Tea?" Ahmed said.

Sty's eyes bulged. Ahmed hastily moved on to saying he thought he'd seen them down at Brains the Breakers: "Last Saturday morning, right? You had a white transit van and there

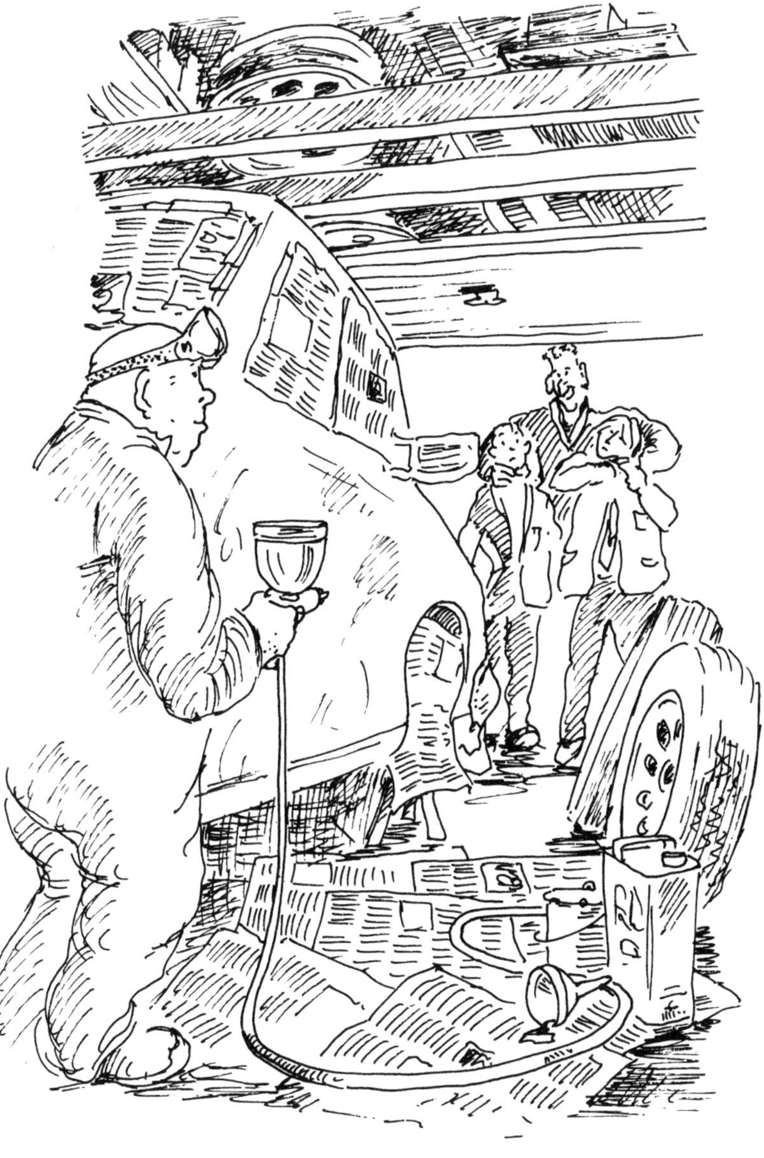

were some wheels in the back."

Sty's hand reached out again, then fell back by his side. "Wheels? Didn't buy any wheels. No wheels in the van, were there, Sully?"

Sully's eyes narrowed, frowning at four alloy wheels leaning against the side wall alongside a rubbish bin with old number plates poking out.

"We had to buy those ones," he said.

"Oh, *those* ones," said Sty. "Yeah, forgot them. But what's it to you?"

Ahmed pulled out his photograph, which was starting to look a bit dog-eared. He showed it to Sty. "That's you."

Sty frowned. There was no doubt about it. Sully was less in focus, though the bumpy bald head was a clue.

"I tell you what," Sty said. "This picture got in the papers!"

We nodded, keeping straight faces.

"But they got it wrong," Sty added, as if confiding some secret, combing bony fingers through his gelled-up hair. "It's very misleading, that picture."

For the first time, I felt slightly hopeful. "We're there in the picture as well, see?" I pointed. "But we weren't there either!"

Sty blinked at me. "Uh?"

Ahmed rushed in to tell him about his Saturday afternoon's work moving tyres at the yard. "And you weren't at that match either," said Ahmed. "But can you say what you were doing?"

Sty was now looking very confused.

Then Sully said, "What Sty meant was, that picture gave us grief, because like, it paints the wrong picture. I mean, if you'd not been there, what would you think? You'd think we were making trouble."

We nodded. It looked that way.

"That's it," Sully said. "The truth is, we were just helping that lad down, because he'd got stuck on the fence."

Ahmed stared at him, baffled.

For once I was quicker than he was. I agreed that Sully and Sty had been helpful, but not at this last match, maybe? "It was a couple of weeks before. At the Everton match," I suggested.

"Oh, yeah," Sty agreed. "We saw that too. Great, that was. That first goal. I mean, it squeezed in by a whisker."

Ahmed got his breath back and said again that maybe that's when the picture had been taken?

"No chance." Sully rubbed his nose. "It was in this week's paper."

"Right," said Sty. "Yeah. That's right. That's what we told the police."

"Police?" I said.

Sully winced. But Ahmed rolled on regardless, repeating why we couldn't have been there, which got Sully grinning again. "He's hoping we'll get his job back with Brains!"

"Yeah, leave it out," Sty gloated. "We've got enough problems, eh, Sully?"

Ahmed gawped like a goldfish. "I tell you, we weren't at this match!"

Sully was grinning away. "Funny, I'd swear I saw you in the row behind us, like it shows in the photo."

Ahmed opened his mouth but no words came out. He was crushed.

"Oh, let's go, Ahmed," I said.

We walked back to Ahmed's house in silence. It was like being caught in a nightmare. None of it made any sense. Or at least, it didn't seem to. What had we missed? Something crucial.

"It mattered to them," I decided. "They needed to prove they were at that match. That's why they didn't want us to say we weren't there."

"But why?" Ahmed said.

"I don't know. But they're in trouble," I said. "They've both been sacked from the Holly Tree Garage, and we were too slow-witted to find out what they did wrong. Perhaps it's connected, somehow. The police were involved. Sty said so."

"You mean, they took the picture down to the newspaper office, because if it got in the paper they'd have a good alibi, Neil?"

I grinned at Ahmed. "That's better!"

"So who snapped the photo then, Neil?"

I frowned. "It must have been someone who gave them the picture. A friend? But they must have needed that alibi really badly, Ahmed, not to mind using a picture that shows what they did to that fan."

"So we need to find out why."

"How can we do that?" I said.

"No problem," said Ahmed. "Dad sells parts to Holly Tree Garage. I'll get him to phone the boss."

7
Phoning the Police

We had to wait until mid-afternoon on the following day to find out why Sty and Sully had been sacked from Holly Tree Garage.

We were in Geography, colouring a map of the Amazon basin green to show how far the rain forests used to stretch twenty years ago and rulering-in red stripes to show how much has been lost since then. It didn't look good on a map and I was trying to imagine what all that cutting and burning might actually look like, when I heard a loud bleeping noise coming from Ahmed's bag.

He pulled out his flash mobile phone. We all groaned. (No one else has one like it.) But Ahmed took no notice, merely twisting it round so I could see it. I read: PHONE DAD.

Ahmed phoned him as soon as lessons were over. The news was a bit of a let-down. Sully and Sty had been fired for using a van from the garage for their own use at weekends, without asking permission. And then getting parking tickets. Last Friday night they'd got three, including one from the police for parking in a bus lane. It wasn't exactly big crime. It wasn't enough to make them go to the trouble of fixing an alibi to throw the police off their trail.

"It doesn't add up," said Ahmed.

"Maybe they've done something else, too. Something much worse."

"Like what?" demanded Ahmed.

"I suppose we could ask the police why they were questioning them."

"You can't do that, Neil, they won't tell you."

I shrugged. "We can only try."

I didn't like the idea of phoning up from home, in case Mum overheard. I wanted to keep this a secret, at least until I'd found out if I was on the right trail. So I phoned the police on my way home. I didn't know quite what to say, and I blurted out about being in the photo in the evening paper with Sty and Sully. The man at the other end asked for my name and address to hand on to the detective working on the case.

Detective? On the case? "But what's the case about?" I asked, nervously.

"I'm sorry, I can't tell you."

I stayed up late that night racking my brains for clues, but nothing made sense. I was stuck – until the following morning, when everything went fast-forward.

* * *

I got back from my paper round to find a police car outside our house. Easing my bike through our gateway, I walked towards the front door. I didn't press the door bell. Instead, I just stood there, staring through the frosted panel at two large men in dark blue uniforms standing in our hallway.

Mum was still wrapped in her bathrobe, but as I took a step back she saw me and opened the door. "Leave your bike outside, Neil," she said and dragged me indoors.

"So this is the man we're after!" said the taller policeman. "We've just been asking your mum what you thought about Arsenal losing last week." He looked at me patiently, but his eyes were watchful. His assistant was shorter and fatter, and looked a bit bored with it all.

"They should have won," I said flatly.

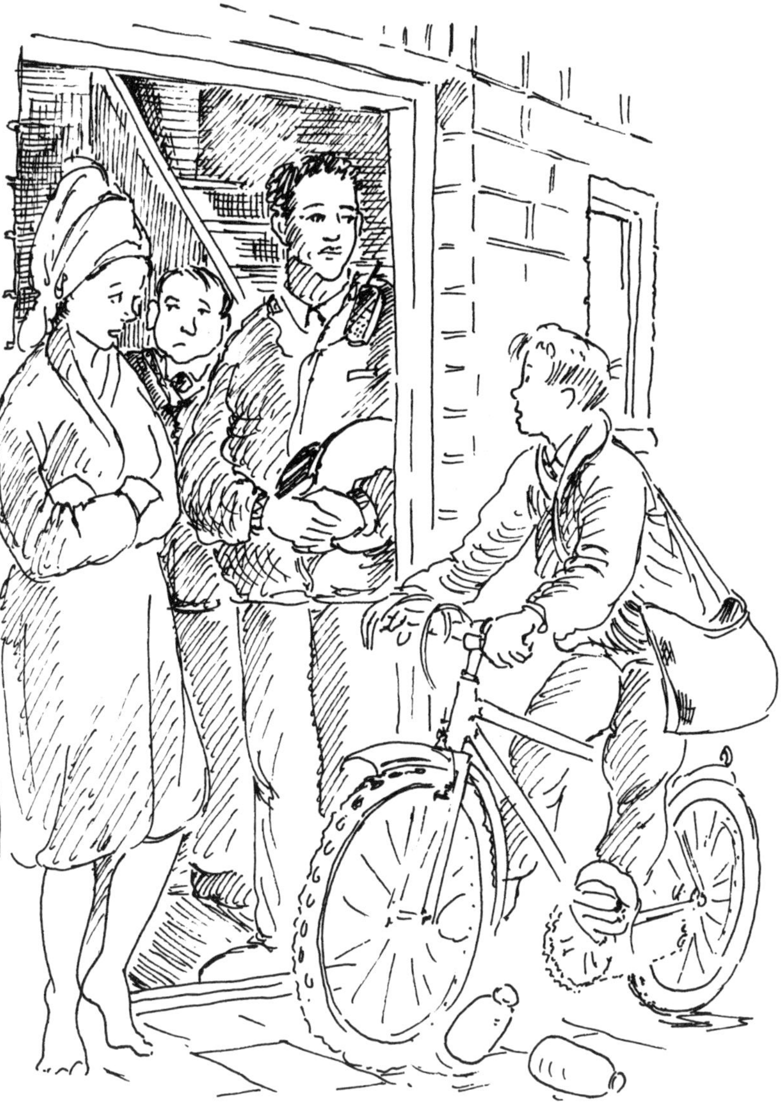

"Except the ref called offside. You could see it was in. There was no doubt—"

"From where you were actually standing?"

"Yes – I mean, no." I understood at last. Mum was watching me coldly. "I only saw the match on the—"

"Nee-ill! In front of these policemen!" She turned to them. "He wasn't like this till he became friends with that Ahmed. Ever since then it's been football and everything else goes out of the window – even the truth—" It all poured out, leaving me stunned. I was gawping. I mean, I did try to speak, but I was shaking so much I don't think I made any sense.

Then the watchful policeman put his hand up at Mum, as if he was stopping a car. She came to a halt at last and I tried to explain everything again.

"I *did* see the match on TV. That's why I phoned the police. I'm sure Sty and Sully can't have been at that match either. Because—"

"Oh, dear," said Mum.

"No, let him have his say, ma'am."

"That picture was taken at the match two weeks earlier. I mean, I can even remember someone with a camera—" A throwaway camera in a bright-yellow cardboard box. It had gone FLASH in my face in the dull light, and someone – I bet it was Sty – had hollered: "Eh, Hezza's snapped us in action!"

"But when we went to see them, they wouldn't admit it," I said, looking at Mum. "They're lying! It's just that I don't know why!"

The tubby policeman kept rolling his cap in his hands like a football, ready to bounce it and give it a bit of a kick. But the watchful one weighed his words: "I ought not to tell you," he said, "but as you've been honest with us, I'll let you into a secret. We think they're lying as well. And we think it's got something to do with the car that crashed into the supermarket last Saturday afternoon."

I stared at him. "They weren't in it?"

He shook his head. "No. And the driver's too badly hurt to tell us why it happened, or where he got the car. But we've talked to his friends and his family and all of them can confirm he'd been saving up to buy himself a car. He had a thousand pounds. That money's now gone missing. We also know that he crashed because his brakes didn't work. That car was a total death trap and the documentation's all false."

I suddenly understood. "He bought it off Sully and Sty!"

"Hold on," said the stocky policeman.

The taller one carried on: "They both deny it. They say someone broke into their garage and stole the keys to the car while they were at the match."

"So that means it was their car?"

"They sort of implied that to start with but then they changed their story. They said it wasn't their car, and that they'd only re-sprayed it for someone. But they couldn't give us the owner's name, or address and so far, this mystery person hasn't dared show his face. The number plates are phoney, so we can't trace him."

"If he exists," I said. "I bet they stole the

car, re-sprayed it, and sold it on Saturday afternoon! That's why they were so anxious to prove they were at the match!"

The policemen glanced at each other, as if to make up their minds whether to shake my hand for being a great detective, or say I was out of my depth. But I was in my stride. I told them about the yellow car in Sully and Sty's garage right now and the odd way they had contradicted each other over whether they'd bought the wheels. Then I saw the stocky policeman wink at the watchful one. I stuttered and stopped.

"I'm sorry." The stocky one didn't look sorry at all. "It's just that we think like you do. But proving it isn't so easy." He held up another copy of that wretched photograph. "We can't break their alibi, see?"

"This photo is their only proof!" I said, staring at it intently.

"That's it."

I'd been wishing for days now that I could think of something to prove to Mum I was telling the truth. Suddenly, I saw it. And it was

63

obvious really. Grabbing hold of the picture, I said: "Look! See my scarf? That's the Arsenal scarf. Ahmed's got one too. And Sty's wearing the Arsenal shirt!"

"Agreed," said the watchful policeman.

"But look at *that* scarf," I cried, indicating the scarf dangling from the neck of the boy half-way up the fence. "Who do those colours belong to?"

The Watchful One looked baffled. "It isn't Arsenal, is it?"

"It's not Man U either! And that's who the Arsenal were playing on Saturday!"

"What does it matter?" Mum broke in.

"It's EVERTON, Mum!" I shouted. "Arsenal were playing against them a couple of weeks ago. That proves when the picture was taken!"

8
Wheels within Wheels

I thought I'd cracked it at last. The policemen sounded impressed. They called me "a smart young lad" and told Mum I ought to go far. But then they went and spoilt it by saying the scarf wasn't proof, not "conclusive proof". It wouldn't be proof in a court of law. It was more like a "useful pointer". On that cheery note they said they had to be off, back to the station.

As soon as the front door closed, I gave Mum a hopeful glance. She looked as if she wasn't sure what to think. "You've been clever, Neil. But even if that photo is from a previous match, you still haven't explained what happened to the free ticket you got from Ahmed's dad."

"Yes, Mum." I needed to move things on.

Perhaps I just had to approach the problem from another way. If I could find more evidence that Sully and Sty were lying, then Ahmed could go back to Brains, and Brains might give him his job back. Ahmed would owe me a favour and maybe he'd come clean with Mum.

I thought about this for a while. I thought of that blue and grey car being sprayed bright yellow. Was that another stolen car they were doing up and hoping to sell? I remembered the bin in the corner, stuffed with old number plates. Would the police be able to trace those? Why hadn't I told them just now?

When I telephoned Ahmed I caught him watching TV, still in bed. He yawned: "I've nothing to do, Neil, now I'm not working for Brains." But he woke up fairly fast when I started to tell him my news.

It wasn't difficult to persuade him to help me. He agreed to meet up as soon as possible, at the corner shop near Burma Mews. Then we could try and have another look inside the Spray Team's garage.

I was there in twenty minutes. Ahmed came ten minutes later, still munching a chocolate muffin. "So, right," he said. "What's it all about?"

"I'll tell you," I said, "if you promise to explain everything to my mum."

"I've already said I can't, Neil."

"If you don't, I'll have no choice. I'll have to talk to your dad. But if you do things my way, you'll get your wages from Brains. You might even get your job back."

He glared at me. "You really reckon so?"

I told him all I knew, which wasn't much,

but at least it gave us a start.

Ahmed got very hopeful. "If we go round to their garage, Neil, you can distract them while I'll try and look in the bin. If I can spot the number off one of those number plates, we could tell the police and they would check it out!"

"OK," I agreed, but before I could work out what I was going to do, a police car swung out from Burma Mews with Sully and Sty in the back. Had they been arrested already? We stared at each other in wonder. What could have brought this about? We carried on into the mews.

The garage doors were half-open. The bright yellow car was still there, standing on new wheels and they weren't just any old wheels. They were the alloys we'd seen last time with thick new treads. It looked like a new machine, but there weren't any number plates on it.

Then a voice from behind said, "Hello there? What can I do for you, Neil?"

We both spun round. I relaxed. It was the

stocky policeman who had come to my house that morning.

"What made you arrest them?" I asked.

He grinned. "You gave us the clue, when you mentioned those wheels. They were stolen. From your headteacher's car!"

* * *

We left the stocky policemen to deal with the fingerprint squad. Ahmed kept exclaiming about how stupid we'd been. "If we'd been quick enough, Neil, we could have claimed the credit, and Hotblack would have been—"

"—amazed. I know," I said with a sigh. "But at least we can go and tell Brains about Sully and Sty. If they've been nicking Hotblack's wheels, they've been up to other tricks, too. That's why they took the photo along to the evening paper, to try and make it look like they were at the match on that afternoon when they sold the car."

"Yeah, Brains will have to believe it! You'll come and back me up, Neil?"

I stopped in my tracks, "One good reason?"

"You owe me."

"*I* owe *you*?"

"For that ticket, Neil. For the match last week."

It was my turn to look like a goldfish. "Your dad paid for that ticket."

"I know, but if you want me to tell your mum the truth, my dad's going to hear about it, and he's going to be so mad. The least I'll have to do is pay back the money he spent on buying our tickets, okay? And how am I going to do that, without my wages from Brains?"

9
Brains at Work

The motor-parts shop was open. Rusty Hinge was at the back, helping a customer with a choice of distributor caps.

"Brains don't want to see you," she called out in her squeaky voice. "We know all about you, Ahmed."

"I'm innocent," Ahmed protested. "And what's more, I've got proof!"

"Proof? Don't think you can fool us."

"I want to see Brains."

"Brains ain't here."

As we backed out of the shed, Ahmed gave

me a helpless look of what-have-I-done-to-deserve-this?

"You've got to try and find Brains. Where else would he be?" I said.

"He's not here all the time, Neil. Last Saturday he was out most of the afternoon. That's why he's not sure where I was."

"But wasn't that woman here, Ahmed?"

"She just stays in the shop and she was still dealing with customers when I went home." He kicked an empty can. It hit the shed with a clang and in the silence that followed, I turned round, scanning the yard. It all looked much the same. Car hell. No doubt about it. And nobody human in sight. Though I could hear a hammering noise, coming from one of the sheds at the back.

"I bet that's Brains," I said. "Come on, we don't want to miss him."

We walked past the motor-parts shop, down a path with the outer fence on one side and the row of sheds on the other. We passed the car crusher, already half-full of wrecks waiting to be flattened and then we reached the last shed. It was the biggest, with a curving metal roof and only a single window, too high up for us to peer through. We walked up to the huge sliding door. The clanking and banging had stopped now. Instead I could hear a loud hissing, and an occasional crackle and roar. It sounded as if somebody was welding.

I banged on the door and the noise stopped. "Brains?" I called. Dogs started barking. "Come on, Brains. We've brought you some news."

A cough from inside. "I don't need news."

"About Sty and Sully?" I tried.

Another short pause. "What about 'em?"

Ahmed closed in behind me. "They've been arrested," he called.

Before he could get any further, Brains was tugging the bolts back. He poked his craggy head out, struggling to keep the dogs back. "What happened? How d'you find out?"

"They do up dud cars," Ahmed said, grinning, "and then sell them! Remember those wheels they showed you? They were stolen. From our head's car. And as for that photo in the paper, it was taken two weeks ago. Sully and Sty just used it to make a false alibi and cover their tracks last Saturday afternoon!"

Silence. Brains seemed to be thinking. It took a long time.

"You owe me," Ahmed persisted.

Brains chewed the inside of his cheek. "You might be making this up."

"Check with the police!"

"Nah, nah..." The caterpillar was squirming, twitching its head and its tail. "I don't want to get... tangled up."

Delving in a back pocket he brought out a fat leather wallet, peeled off four or five notes and shoved them at Ahmed. "All right? All over and done with. You're lucky I'm feeling generous. Now, scarper. I'm busy, okay?"

"So can I have my job back?"

Brains pulled the door shut in our faces.

Ahmed was licking his lips, stuffing the notes in his pocket, but I felt a sense of letdown, as if we'd been cheated. "I still don't think I get this."

"No, but I do. Thirty quid."

"But... how did he know their names?"

"Who, Sully and Sty? We told him."

"Only just now," I pointed out. "Before we'd said anything else, he knew who we were talking about. He was rattled by something. What's he up to now?"

From the shed came a quite different noise. Iron chains were being dragged over the concrete floor. I tried to find some chink or crack in the door but there weren't any, and the only way to see through that high window was by finding something to stand on. A ladder, for instance. No luck. The only way I could do it would be if I could climb on those wrecks stacked up in the car crusher.

In fact it was easy enough, using the broken windows and axles and bonnets as steps, even though all the cars started tilting and creaking under my feet. I wormed my way in through the open door of the third car in the stack, an upside down transit van with all its windows intact, and crawled along the inside. Peering out of the windscreen, I got the view I was after.

Brains was rushing around inside the shed. He was moving gear on trolleys. He seemed to be clearing away. Then he dragged the door open and peered out, left and right, as if to check we'd gone before hurrying into the yard. The dogs bounded out behind him,

putting their noses down to sniff all over the place before locking into our scent and heading straight for the car crusher.

I should have been worried by this, but I was even more disturbed by what I could see through the doorway. A car was inside the garage. It had a green bonnet, blue wings, and an orange roof, with blackened bits all down the seams. It had obviously been welded together. But why were there chains looped round it?

I wondered what Ahmed thought, but he was down below, sounding panicky. An

Alsatian was sniffing his boots. "I can't stand dogs! Get it off me."

"It's not going to bite," I said.

Then the dog growled, and Ahmed was scrambling up the cars. The whole stack wobbled and tilted even further forward and I shouted to him to be careful. He just blurted out that he he'd got to get away from the dogs. He made it to the van and pulled the door shut.

All of a sudden, we both heard a low whining sound and cough-cough, chug-chug-chug. It was an engine being cranked into action somewhere across the yard. We stared through the upside down windscreen and in a few moments we saw a rusty old yellow monster with caterpillar tracks rumbling slowly towards us. Its funnel spewed out black fumes. On the back was a long steel arm, doubled up like one of Brains' elbows, with a giant steel claw on the end. The dogs circled round, snarling at it. The ground was rumbling now. The cars in the stack were trembling.

"What's Brains up to?" I shouted.

The bulldozer trundled past at about two miles an hour, and stopped by the open door of the shed. Brains twisted round in the cab and started juggling some levers. The steel arm opened, stretched, and swung round into the shed and over the top of the car. The claw came down on its roof. Then Brains was out of the cab, leaving the engine juddering, hurrying round to the car, and attaching the chains to the claw. He jumped back in the cab and started pulling his levers again.

The claw jerked up. The car tilted, lifting off the ground and swaying out into the yard. Up it went, higher and higher, until it was higher than we were. Then the bulldozer started reversing. The car disappeared overhead. CRASH! We bounced in the air. The car was on top of the van.

The claw arm swung back with chains dangling. The bulldozer roared and cut out. Brains walked across to the crusher.

"Oh, no!" Ahmed gasped, "I don't believe this!"

I did. It was all making sense. But before I could think about it, let alone try to explain, *Bzzzzzzzzzzzzzzz–ccl-cl, ccl-cl–*

"We've got to get out!"

"But the dogs are down there!" Ahmed wailed.

"D'you want to get crushed?"

Ahmed turned, and his eyes were like saucers. "This door's stuck!"

I tried the other door, but the car crashing down on top must have jammed both the locks. I crawled back through the van, intending to force the rear doors, only to see that they were squeezed against the black iron girders at the back of the crushing machine.

Then the concrete block crashed down.

We were both bounced in the air like rag dolls. I banged my head and came down stretched on my side. Then everything wobbled and wavered, and we were both rolling into each other, then slithering far apart as the van jerked up and down. Its panelling started to buckle, bending out on both sides with a horrible rending screech so

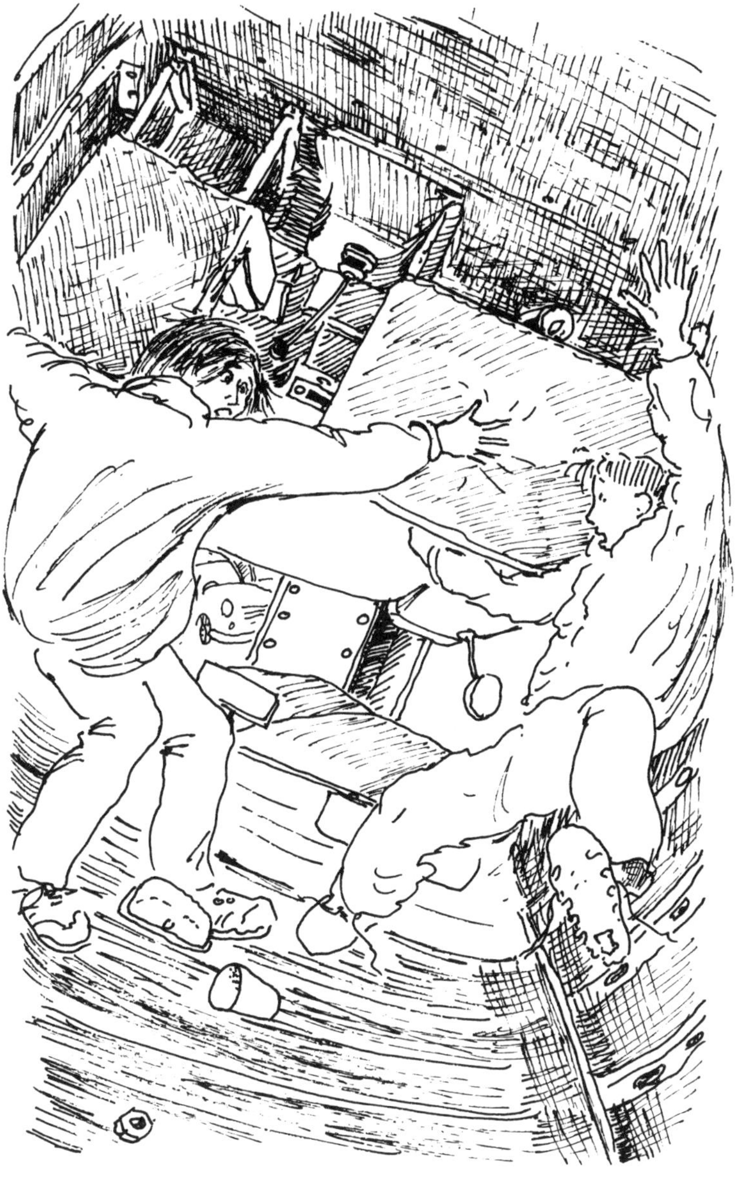

loud it hurt my ears, but I didn't care about that. I was stupidly trying to stand up, trying to put my hands on the upturned floor overhead, as if I could stop the thing squashing down.

Then CRUNCH! I was pitched to one side, hitting my elbows and knees, and the windscreen smashed into smithereens, sending a cascade of glass shooting through the air, stinging my hands and face and pinging into the metal. The van heaved and bucked. It convulsed.

We were both hopelessly screaming against all that deafening din, our mouths and eyes full of dust as the floor and the ceiling wrenched closer, fraction by terrible fraction until even lying down I could touch them both. I had the mad thought that we were going to end up as a very thin meaty filling, spread in a metal sandwich. No one would ever find us.

10
Sully and Sty Give a Hand

Suddenly, everything stopped. No juddering. No more shrinking. I could hear myself screaming. Or was that just inside my head? My mouth was still open. I closed it. I found myself looking at Ahmed, only a fraction away, and he was blinking and rubbing his eyes. The dust was bitter and sharp and I could hear something dripping. I knew what that was. I sniffed petrol. And from somewhere further away, I started to hear other noises. Odd squeaks and slitherings and bumps.

Then I heard Brains. "Hello, lads! (Was he calling to us? No, he wasn't.) Those stupid boys came round here and told me you'd been arrested!"

Sty answered sullenly, "Thanks to you."

"Me?" Brains said. "Come off it! I didn't give nothing away, not even your names. Okay?"

"No, Brains, it's not okay." This was Sully speaking. "You broke into our garage and took the keys of that rotten car you'd welded together. Shame you'd forgotten to tell us you'd found a punter to buy it. Then you spotted that photo our mate Hezza took at the Everton match, pinched it off the wall and sold it to the paper. Too clever by half, weren't you, Brains?"

"I only did it to give you an alibi, Sully, to prove you were at the match. To prove you couldn't have sold that car—"

"You did it because you were scared that if the police caught us, we just might have told them that it was YOU that sold the car."

Sty glared at Brains. "That boy who was

working for you. He knew you weren't at the yard on Saturday afternoon, so he could have got you in trouble. But not if you could make it look like he'd been with us at the match instead!"

"I was trying to look after all of us. I mean, we're a team!"

Sully grinned coldly. "Not now, Brains. We lied to the police when we told them we didn't know who owned the car we'd sprayed. But that left us as prime suspects, even before those boys came round and saw their teacher's wheels. So, one way or other, we ended up getting the blame for everything, including cobbling together old wrecks and selling 'em with false papers. That's not fair, is it, Brains? When all we've done is re-spray 'em, entirely on your behalf."

"So we've come clean," said Sty.

"You *what*?" Brains' voice nearly snapped.

By now I was leaning out through the broken windscreen, so I saw a line of policemen moving out from behind the bulldozer. Brains saw them a moment later.

"I'm innocent," Brains whined. "You can't pin nothing on me."

"Soon will though," Sully said, "when they see what you've got in your shed. Another old cobbled-up wreck for some kid with more money than sense."

Sty and the police rushed into the shed. "Hey, Sully. It's disappeared!" Sty hollered anxiously.

Brains grinned at the policemen. "There's nothing in there. Never has been. These two are just trying to frame me."

"Liar!" Sty screamed.

"You can't prove it!"

"*We* can!" Ahmed and I both shouted at once.

Everyone looked up, wide-eyed, as if they'd just heard a ghost. Ahmed added, quite calmly: "The proof is on top of our heads."

11
Explanations

Slowly everything began to sort itself out. Sty and Sully were still in trouble for stealing Mr Hotblack's alloy wheels (and probably other things, too). Brains was also arrested, and charged with selling vehicles under false pretences.

Ahmed had to explain everything to his dad. To start with, his dad was furious that Ahmed had lied to him. "Don't expect any more, pocket money – and you're grounded," he yelled. "For a month!" But when Ahmed didn't argue, his dad gave a twitch of a grin.

"OK. You've learned a lesson not to climb into car crushers, Ahmed," he said, "and I can't say I'm too unhappy that Brains is out of the way." He grinned more broadly at me. "I'm just very glad you both got out of this alive." Then Ahmed and his dad came round and talked to Mum.

Mum realised she'd made a mistake. I don't want to gloat about this, but she told me how sorry she was. I was so relieved the whole thing was over that I said, "Don't worry, forget it." And we gave each other a big hug. Then we all went out together, down to the pizzeria, and had an incredible evening.

* * *

I thought life had got back to normal until Monday afternoon, when I came home from school and got the horrible feeling I was back in the previous week. Mum's car was parked outside but when I called out, "Hi, Mum," she didn't answer. I went into the kitchen, and there she was, reading the evening paper.

"Mum?"

Silence.

I looked over her shoulder at two photos on an inside page. The first showed Ahmed and me at that football match, with Sully and Sty cut out. The second one showed Mr Hotblack, standing beside his Ford Escort. The headline read:

SCHOOLBOY DETECTIVES TRACK
DOWN HEAD'S STOLEN WHEELS

Mum looked round. She was beaming.

"It isn't exactly the truth, Mum."

She actually chuckled out loud. "I don't think we'll worry about that. Your head's just been on the phone, practically singing your praises. I'm very proud of you, Neil!"

About the author

I grew up in Surrey and Kent, graduating in history from Sussex University. Since then, I have worked in a cake-mix factory, a hotel and a museum; started a restaurant, imported wine and rebuilt an old farmhouse in Italy.

I have written many books for children and I also work as an artist.

The idea for *Car Crusher* came from helping a friend, whose 1960s Citroen had conked out once too often. We had to tow the old car to a scrapyard where it ended its days on top of a rusty milk float.

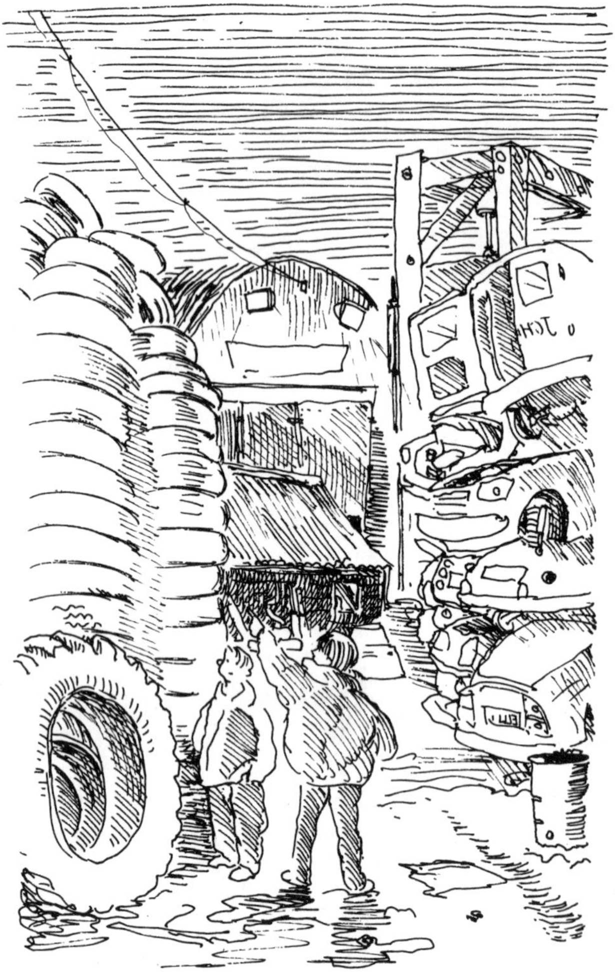